T0347498

bush theatre

The Bush Theatre presents the world premiere of

FEAR

by Dominic Savage

19 June - 14 July 2012

Sponsored by Ogilvy & Mather

With thanks to
Westfield, Dwell, Jo Topping, Mark Dakin, Andy Hilton
at Belgrade Theatre Company, Daniele Lydon, Suzanne Bell,
Matthew Byam Shaw, Hamleys, Richard James (Savile Row),
Lisa Duncan, Andrew Taylor at Duran Audio, Stage Electrics,
Smythson of Bond Street, Ella May Mcdermott, Zoe Spurr,
Lisa Duncan, William Gilchrist, Stefan Furenbrink
& Will Adams at Rake and Sian Breckin

Cast and Creative Team

Amanda | **Louise Delamere**
Gerald | **Rupert Evans**
Jason | **Jason Maza**
Kieran | **Aymen Hamdouchi**
Kieran's Mum | **Lorna Brown**

Writer and Director – Dominic Savage
Designer – takis
Lighting Designer – James Whiteside
Sound Designer and Composer – Ed Clarke
Casting Director – Chloe Emmerson
Company Stage Manager – Mary Hely
Assistant Stage Manager – Sarah Barnes
Assistant Stage Manager (placement) – Susan Fayyad
Costume Supervisor – Sara Polonghini
Set Builder – Foot Print
Production Assistant – Jamie Robson
Production Electrician – Nic Farman

Company

Lorna Brown Kieran's Mum

Theatre includes: *Clybourne Park* (Royal Court and Wyndhams Theatre); *Short Fuses* (Bristol Old Vic); *Once on This Island* (Hackney Empire & Tour); *Things of Dry Hours* (Royal Exchange & Gate Theatre); *93.2FM* (Royal Court); *Trade* (RSC); *The Big Life*, *Funny Black Women on the Edge* (Stratford East) *The Weave* (Soho).

Television includes: Dominic Savage's *True Love*, *Outnumbered*, *Much Ado About Nothing*, *French and Saunders*, *Family Business*, *Rough Treatment*, *Bad Girls*, *Catherine Tate Show*, *Vivienne Vyle*, *Holby City*, *Casualty*, *Coronation Street* and *The Bill*.

Film includes: *Les Misérables*, *World War Z*, *Gambit*, *Little Soldier*.

Louise Delamere Amanda

Theatre includes: *Suddenly Last Summer* (Nottingham Playhouse); *Tartuffe* (Royal Exchange, Manchester); *Cyrano de Bergerac* (Haymarket, Theatre Royal); *Love and Liberty* (Tron Glasgow); *Hayfever* (The Royal Edinburgh Lyceum); *The Beggar's Opera* (Traverse Theatre).

Recent television includes: *The Bible*, *Vexed*, *Scott & Bailey*, *Waterloo Road*, *The Good Samaritan*, *Doc Martin*, *Torchwood*, *The Rise and Fall of Rome*, *The Chatterley Affair*, *No Angels*, *People Like Us*, *Dirty War*.

Film includes: *The List*, *U Want Me 2 Kill Him*, *A Boy Called Dad*, *Bullet Boys*, *Daddy's Girl*, *Family Business*, *Born Romantic*, *Mad Dogs and Englishmen*, *Princess Caraboo*, *Judge Dredd*.

Rupert Evans Gerald

Theatre for the Bush includes *Physco geography* and *His Ghostly Heart*; (The Broken Space Season).

Other theatre includes: *Life is a Dream*, *Kiss of the Spiderwoman* (Donmar Warehouse); *Romeo and Juliet*, *King John* (RSC); *Breathing Corpses* (Royal Court); *Sweet Panic* (Duke of York's Theatre).

Television includes: *World Without End*, *The Little House*, *Emma*, *Monday Monday*, *The Palace*, *A Midsummer Night's Dream*, *Fingersmith*, *North and South* and *Sons and Lovers*.

Film includes: *The Incident*, *Elfie Hopkins*, *Sidney Turtlebaum*, *Agora*, *Guantanamera*, *Otto* and *Hellboy*.

Aymen Hamdouchi Kieran

Television includes: Dominic Savage's *True Love*, *Black Mirror: The National Anthem*.

Film includes: *Offender*, *My Brother The Devil*, *Zero Dark Thirty*, *Laid Off*, *Ghost*, *Some Dogs Bite*.

Jason Maza Jason

Theatre for the Bush includes *Flight Path*.

Other theatre includes: *Sucker Punch* (Royal Court); *Pornography* (Tricycle Theatre); *Mad Blud* (Theatre Royal Stratford East).

Television includes: *Silk*, *Whitechapel*, *The Titanic* and *Trial & Retribution*; and for film, *Get Lucky*, *The Man Inside*, *Welcome to the Punch*, *Outside Bet*, *The Knot*, *Victim*, *Demons Never Die*, *Shifty* and *Fish Tank*.

Dominic Savage Writer and Director

Dominic began his career as a documentary film maker. His documentary work for television includes a number of films made for Channel 4 - *Seaside Organist* for the Short Story strand, *The Outsiders* (nominated for the Grierson award) and *Rogue Males & The Complainers* for *Cutting Edge*. He has also made a number of documentaries for the BBC.

In 2000 Savage turned to fiction and wrote and directed *Nice Girl* for BBC Drama winning the BAFTA Award for New Director Fiction 2001. *Nice Girl* was also nominated for Best Single Drama and Innovation at the BAFTA Television Awards 2001.

He then wrote and directed *When I Was 12* in 2001 for BBC Screen Two, winning the BAFTA Award for Best Single Film. Then came *Out of Control* in 2002 (BBC One), winning the Michael Powell Award for Best British Film at the Edinburgh Film Festival 2002 and the Royal Television Society Award, and Broadcast awards for Best Single Film 2003.

LOVE + HATE was Savage's first feature. Released Nationwide in May 2006, the film premièred at the Berlin Film Festival in 2005, winning awards at Giffoni, Palm Springs, Malmo, and Ziln Film Festivals.

Single dramas *Born Equal* (BBC One) starring Colin Firth, Anne Marie Duff, and Robert Carlyle and *Freefall* (BBC Two) starring Dominic Cooper, Anna Maxwell Martin, and Aiden Gillan followed.

In 2010 He wrote a two-part television drama with Simon Stephens that he directed for BBC Two called *Dive*.

Savage's latest work for television is a semi-improvised five-part drama series entitled *True Love*, all shot in his home town of Margate, for BBC One, due to be screened in June.

takis Designer

takis is an experimental set, costume and installation designer. He was nominated for a 2012 Off West End Theatre Award for *His Teeth*. From 2007-2011 as Designer in residence for HighTide takis built the visual identity of the company, designing diverse productions to great acclaim including the very successful *Stovepipe* in collaboration with the National Theatre (Off West End Design nomination), *Ditch* with Old Vic and Lidless (Fringe First Award winner in Edinburgh Festival 2010). takis is also the artistic director of his own company Artluxe, which produces installation and performance art. Theatre includes: *Bacchae* (Royal & Derngate); *Napoli* (West Yorkshire Playhouse & tour); *Denial* (King's Head Theatre); *Clytemnestra* (Sherman Theatre); *His Teeth* (Only Connect); *As You Like It & Merlin* (Chester Open Air Theatre*); Nicked, Midnight Your Time & Dusk Rings a Bell* (HighTide/Edinburgh Festival); *Measure for Measure* (Sherman Theatre); *Oh! What a Lovely War* (RADA); *Much Ado About Nothing & Hercules* (Chester Open Air Theatre); *Ditch* (Old Vic/HighTide), *Lidless* (HighTide & Edinburgh Festival), *The Early Bird* (Finborough Theatre/Project Art Centre-Dublin), *Signs of a Star Shaped Diva* (Theatre Royal Stratford East & National Tour), *Stovepipe* (National Theatre/HighTide), *The Marriage Bed* (Hong Kong/ NY); *Invasion* (Soho Theatre); *I Caught Crabs in Walberswick* (Bush Theate & Edinburgh Festival); *Scenes from the Big Picture* (RADA); *Crazy Lady* (Drill Hall & Contact Theatre Manchester).

Installations include: *Forgotten Peacock* (Design Museum/The Brunswick); *Installation 496* (RADA), *Goldfish* (Paris Fashion Week); *Mythological Installation Oedipus* (Bucharest Museum of Contemporary Art); *Visual Performance in Baroque Spirit* (Venice Carnival).

Music Performances includes: *Dick Whittington* (Gatehouse Theatre), *Nicked* (HighTide Festival), *A Tale of Two Cities* (Theatre Royal Brighton), *Bloodbath* (Edinburgh Festival), *Maria Callas – Vissi D'arte, Vissi D'amore* (Barbican); *Choruses* (Ancient Epidaurus/ Frankfurt); *The Words of Love* (Athens*); In the Light of the Night* (Ancient Epidaurus); *Nikos Skalkotas* (Queen Elizabeth Hall).

Film includes: *Dreck* (feature film), *Half Light* (short film), *Eve* (short film).

www.takis.info

Ed Clarke Sound Designer and Composer

Ed was nominated for an Olivier Award for his sound design for Danny Boyle's *Frankenstein* (Olivier, National Theatre); other sound designs include: *Backbeat* (Duke of York's Theatre); *The Mysteries* and *The Good Hope* (Cottesloe, National Theatre); *The Railway Children* (Waterloo International Station and Roundhouse Theatre Toronto); *His Teeth* (Only Connect Theatre); *The Wiz* (Birmingham Rep and West Yorkshire Playhouse); *Baby Doll* (Albery Theatre); *Alex* (Arts Theatre, UK and international tour); *Happy Now?* (Hull Truck Theatre); *Old Times, A Doll's House* (Donmar Warehouse); *Bad Man Christmas* (HMP Wormwood Scrubs); *The Wizard Of Oz* and *Sandi Toksvig's Christmas Cracker* (Royal Festival Hall); *Singular Sensations* (Haymarket Theatre); *Twelfth Night, Slice of Saturday Night* (Queen's Theatre Hornchurch); *Moti Roti Puttli Chunni, Running Dream* and Mike Leigh's *It's A Great Big Shame,* (Theatre Royal Stratford East); *The Milk Train Doesn't Stop Here Anymore, Treasure Island, The Cabinet of Doctor Caligari, Kindertotenlieder, Then Again, Angela Carter's Cinderella, Cause Célèbre, Mrs Warren's Profession, A Midsummer Night's Dream* (Lyric Theatre Hammersmith).

As Associate Sound Designer credits include: Matthew Bourne's *Early Adventures* (UK tour); *Mary Poppins* (UK national tour, Circustheater Scheveningen and current US tour), *My Fair Lady* (UK and US national tours), *Acorn Antiques* (UK national tour), *The Witches* (UK national tour), *Return To The Forbidden Planet* (UK national tour), *Soul Train* (UK tour).

Ed also tours as front-of-house sound engineer for *Van der Graaf Generator,* and has previously toured with *Ryuichi Sakamoto, Blue Man Group, The John Tams Band, Evelyn Glennie,* and *Talvin Singh.*

Forthcoming projects include: *Blue Man Group* (Monte Carlo theatre, Las Vegas).

James Whiteside Lighting Designer

West End credits include: *Midnight Tango* (Aldwych); *Never Forget* (Savoy); *Footloose* (Novello and Playhouse); *Holding The Man* (Trafalgar Studios); *The Female Of The Species* (Vaudeville); Calamity Jane (Shaftesbury).

Other recent credits include: *A Marvellous Year For Plums, The Ragged Trousered Philanthropists, Wallenstein, Funny Girl, The Lion, The Witch And The Wardrobe, Alice In Wonderland, The Snow Queen* (Chichester Festival Theatre); *Moonlight And Magnolias* and *Twelfth Night* (Perth Theatre); *A Christmas Carol, Arcadia, Grimm Tales, Gates Of Gold* (Library, Manchester); *The Absence Of Women* (Lyric, Belfast); *A Voyage Round My Father* (Salisbury Playhouse); *Love's Labour's Lost* (The Rose, Kingston); *Salonika* (West Yorkshire Playhouse); *Animal Farm* (Bath Theatre Royal); *Monkee Business* (Manchester Opera House); *Transparency, This Piece Of Earth* and *The Early Bird* (Ransom Productions, Belfast); *Over The Bridge* (Waterfront Hall, Belfast); *Jump!* (Live Theatre, Newcastle) and *As You Like It* (Grosvenor Park Open Air Theatre, Chester).

For Tall Stories Theatre Company credits include: *The Gruffalo, The Gruffalo's Child, Room On The Broom, The Snail And The Whale, Mr Benn* and *Snow White.*

Forthcoming productions include: *The Odd Couple* (Perth Theatre); *James And The Giant Peach* (Birmingham Stage Company).

bush theatre

About the Bush Theatre

The Bush Theatre is a world-famous home for new plays and an internationally renowned champion of playwrights and artists. Since its inception in 1972, the Bush has pursued its singular vision of discovery, risk and entertainment from a distinctive corner of West London. Now located in a recently renovated library building on the Uxbridge Road in the heart of Shepherds Bush, the theatre houses a 144-seat auditorium, rehearsal rooms and a lively café bar.

www.bushtheatre.co.uk

At the Bush Theatre

The Bush Theatre
7 Uxbridge Road
London, W12 8LJ
Box Office: 020 8743 5050
Administration: 020 8743 3584
email: info@bushtheatre.co.uk

The Alternative Theatre Company Ltd (The Bush Theatre) is a registered charity and a company limited by guarantee.

Registered in England No. 1221968. Charity No. 270080

THANK YOU
TO OUR SUPPORTERS

The Bush Theatre would like to extend a very special 'Thank You' to the following Patrons, Corporate Supporters and Trusts & Foundations whose valuable contributions continue to help us nurture, develop and present some of the brightest new literary stars and theatre artists.

LONE STAR
Gianni Alen-Buckley
Michael Alen-Buckley
Francois & Julie Buclez
Siri & Rob Cope
Jonathan Ford & Susannah Herbert
Catherine Johnson
Caryn Mandabach
Miles Morland
Lady Susie Sainsbury
James & Virginia Turnbull
Nicholas & Francesca Whyatt

HANDFUL OF STARS
Anonymous
Jim Broadbent
Philip & Tita Byrne
Sarah Cooke
Clyde Cooper
David & Alexandra Emmerson
Catherine Faulks
Chris & Sofia Fenichell
Kate Groes
Nicolette Kirkby
Mark & Sophie Lewisohn
Adrian & Antonia Lloyd
Eugenie White & Andrew Loewenthal
Peter & Bettina Mallinson
Paige Nelson
Georgia Oetker
Bianca Roden
Claudia Rossler
Naomi Russell
Charles & Emma Sanderson
Eva Sanchez-Ampudia & Cyrille Walter
Joana & Henrik Schliemann
Jon & NoraLee Sedmak
Larus Shields
Trish Wadley
Charlotte & Simon Warshaw
John & Amelia Winter

RISING STARS
Anonymous
Nick Balfour
Tessa Bamford
David Bernstein & Sophie Caruth
Simon Berry
John Bottrill
David Brooks
Karen Brost
Maggie Burrows
Clive Butler
Matthew Byam Shaw
Benedetta Cassinelli
Tim & Andrea Clark
Claude & Susie Cochin de Billy

Angela Cole
Matthew Cushen
Irene Danilovich
Michael & Marianne de Giorgio
Yvonna Demczynska
Jane & David Fletcher
Lady Antonia Fraser
Vivien Goodwin
Sarah Griffin
Hugh & Sarah Grootenhuis
Mr & Mrs Jan Gustafsson
Martin & Melanie Hall
Sarah Hall
Giselle Hantz
Hugo & Julia Heath
Urs & Alice Hodler
Bea Hollond
Zaza Jabre
Simon Johnson
Ann & Ravi Joseph
Davina & Malcolm Judelson
Paul & Cathy Kafka
Rupert Jolley & Aine Kelly
Kristen Kennish
Tarek & Diala Khlat
Heather Killen
Sue Knox
Neil LaBute
Isabella Macpherson
Caroline Mackay
Charlie & Polly McAndrew
Michael McCoy
Judith Mellor
Roger Miall
David & Anita Miles
Caro Millington
Pedro & Carole Neuhaus
Kate Pakenham
Mark & Anne Paterson
Julian & Amanda Platt
Lila Preston
Radfin Courier Service
Kirsty Raper
Clare Rich
Joanna Richards
Sarah Richards
Robert Rooney
Karen Scofield & LUCZA
Russ Shaw & Lesley Hill
Saleem & Alexandra Siddiqi
Melanie Slimmon
Brian Smith
William Smith-Bowers
Sebastian & Rebecca Speight
Nick Starr
Andrew & Emma Sutcliffe
The Uncertainty Principle
Ed Vaizey

Marina Vaizey
The van Tulleken family
Francois & Arelle von Hurter
Hilary Vyse & Mark Ellis
Amanda Waggott
Dame Harriet Walter
Peter Wilson-Smith & Kat Callo
Alison Winter
Jessica Zambeletti

CORPORATE SUPPORTERS

SPOTLIGHT
John Lewis, Park Royal

LIGHTBULB
The Agency (London) Ltd
AKA
Mozzo Coffee & La Marzocco
Talk Talk Ltd
The Bush would also like to thank Markson Pianos, Westfield and West 12 Shopping & Leisure Centre

TRUSTS AND FOUNDATIONS
The Andrew Lloyd Webber Foundation
The Daisy Trust
The D'Oyly Carte Charitable Trust
EC&O Venues Charitable Trust
The Elizabeth & Gordon Bloor Charitable Foundation
Foundation for Sport and the Arts
Garfield Weston Foundation
Garrick Charitable Trust
The Gatsby Charitable Foundation
The Goldsmiths' Company
The Grocers' Charity
The Harold Hyam Wingate Foundation
Jerwood Charitable Foundation
The John Thaw Foundation
The Laurie & Gillian Marsh Charitable Trust
The Leverhulme Trust
The Martin Bowley Charitable Trust
The Hon M J Samuel Charitable Trust
The Thistle Trust
Sir Siegmund Warburg's Voluntary Settlement

If you are interested in finding out how to be involved, please visit the 'Support Us' section of www.bushtheatre.co.uk, or call 020 8743 3584

bushgreen

bushgreen is a social-networking website for people in theatre to connect, collaborate and publish plays in innovative ways. Our mission is to connect playwrights with theatre practitioners and plays with producers, to promote best practice and inspire the creation of exciting new theatre. bushgreen allows members to:

- Submit plays directly to the Bush for our team to read and consider for production

- Connect with other writers, directors, producers and theatres

- Publish scripts online so more people can access your work

- Read scripts from hundreds of new playwrights

There are thousands of members and hundreds of plays on the site.

To join, log on to www.bushgreen.org

FEAR

Dominic Savage

FEAR

OBERON BOOKS
LONDON

WWW.OBERONBOOKS.COM

First published in 2012 by Oberon Books Ltd
521 Caledonian Road, London N7 9RH
Tel: +44 (0) 20 7607 3637 / Fax: +44 (0) 20 7607 3629
e-mail: info@oberonbooks.com
www.oberonbooks.com

A catalogue record for this book is available from the British Library.

PB ISBN: 978-1-84943-420-1
Digital ISBN: 978-1-84943-603-8

Cover design by Analogue

Visit www.oberonbooks.com to read more about all our books
and to buy them. You will also find features, author interviews and
news of any author events, and you can sign up for e-newsletters
so that you're always first to hear about our new releases.

Characters

AMANDA

GERALD

JASON

KIERAN

KIERAN'S MUM

This text went to press before the end of rehearsals
and so may differ slightly from the play as performed.

KIERAN AND MUM

KIERAN is on the couch asleep. It is morning. His MUM enters, waking him.

MUM: Kieran? Kieran.

KIERAN wakes up.

KIERAN: Yeah mum.

MUM: You going down jobseekers?

KIERAN: Yeah mum, yeah.

MUM: What time you supposed to be there?

KIERAN: Nine.

MUM: It's 8 o'clock, get up. Get up man.

KIERAN doesn't move.

Get up!

KIERAN sits up. MUM sits at the kitchen table.

How's it all going?

KIERAN: Alright.

MUM: Is that it? Alright? Is that all you've got to say?

KIERAN: I've been writing my CV. Doing lots of job applications, just have to see what comes up.

MUM: I need some money from you.

KIERAN: I've only got a score.

MUM: That'll do.

KIERAN gives her the money.

You're not fucking around are you?

KIERAN: No.

MUM: You promise me?

KIERAN: I promise.

MUM: Hope you get a job soon, that will sort you out.

KIERAN: I'm trying mum.

MUM: Give me a light.

KIERAN lights his MUM's cigarette.

It's good what's happening with you, you know, I'm pleased with you, pleased with what's going on.

KIERAN: Yeah, well. It's hard though.

MUM: I honestly don't know what would have happened to you if you'd carried on you know.

KIERAN: Dead or prison?

MUM: That's the truth. Have you found yourself a girlfriend?

KIERAN: No.

MUM: That would help you know. You should.

KIERAN: Yeah well. Don't trust you lot.

MUM: What?

KIERAN: Too much maintenance.

They laugh together about this.

MUM: You and me are working better too.

KIERAN: We are.

MUM gets up.

MUM: I'm pleased we got through that bad time, very pleased.

KIERAN: Me too.

MUM: I like it just simple. Peaceful. That's all I want. There's nothing wrong with that you know, in life. Something simple. Just getting through.

KIERAN: Yeah I know.

MUM: You keep doing good, staying out of trouble. I know it's hard, but you have to. I've told you before, what comes around goes around.

KIERAN: *(In unison.)* What comes around goes around.

MUM: What time you back?

KIERAN: 7/8 p.m.

MUM: Make sure it's 7. OK.

MUM leaves.

KIERAN sees that she's gone and gets on the phone. He talks in a very different way. Harsh.

KIERAN: Jas, you coming over? We've got fucking business to do. Make it about 12. Cool, see you then. Don't be late.

KIERAN has made the bed. KIERAN is sat at the table. MUM leaves out of the front. AMANDA enters from behind and sits on the bed. Lights fade down on KIERAN, lights fade up on AMANDA.

GERALD AND AMANDA'S HOME

GERALD works in the city.

An investment banker.

He has everything going for him. GERALD is making money, he has a great lifestyle, and there's much to look forward to.

He is married to AMANDA. AMANDA is pregnant with their first child.

GERALD comes in. AMANDA is sat at the kitchen table.

AMANDA: Morning.

GERALD: Morning. You're up early?

GERALD goes to AMANDA and kisses her.

How are you feeling?

AMANDA: I'm not sleeping that well.

GERALD: Really?

AMANDA: I keep getting up to pee.

GERALD: I didn't hear you.

AMANDA: It's normal, apparently. Something to do with high levels of progesterone. God, I've never felt so tired.

AMANDA smiles though, she's happy.

GERALD: Coffee?

AMANDA: No thanks, I've got a herbal tea.

GERALD has his morning routine, he's constantly checking his Blackberry, distracted by his Financial Times, but at the same time able to attend to AMANDA.

Feels like a fish is swimming around in my belly.

GERALD: Oh.

AMANDA: Apparently it all gets better in the second trimester.

GERALD: That's good.

AMANDA: Hopefully I'll finally stop feeling nauseous then as well.

GERALD takes hold of AMANDA's hand.

GERALD: You know, we need to do as much going away as we can, while we can. We should take advantage of this time. We really should. It would be good for us to.

AMANDA: You can still travel with a small baby you know. I know lots of people who do.

GERALD: I'm talking about now, about you and me time. It will be different you know, when there's three of us. It will never be just you and me again. I thought about that the other day. What with what's going on at work, I need a break, we both need one.

AMANDA: You're right.

GERALD: I know I am. We haven't been to Bab Al Shams for a while.

AMANDA: Dubai?

GERALD: We need pampering, we need some serious pampering.

AMANDA: Can you be bothered with the flight? Six hours isn't it.

GERALD: It'll be worth it. I promise. They've got it so sorted out there. I need that level of service. God I do.

AMANDA: What about somewhere like the Hermitage?

GERALD: Monaco.

GERALD gets hold of his iPad.

AMANDA: We've always enjoyed it there.

GERALD: Maybe.

AMANDA: I'd prefer the shorter flight.

GERALD smiles with a memory.

GERALD: There's always Venice?

AMANDA: The Gritti Palace.

GERALD: Remember that dinner?

AMANDA: That was an amazing week.

GERALD: It really was.

AMANDA: Should we though? It would never be the same, would it?

GERALD: We could try to somehow recapture it?

AMANDA: I don't know.

GERALD: Come on, it's a good idea. I'll see what I can find.

AMANDA: It would be lovely.

GERALD looks at his watch.

GERALD: I should get going.

AMANDA: You know we've got the scan this week?

GERALD: Yeah that's right.

AMANDA: Wednesday at 11. You have taken the morning off haven't you?

GERALD: Of course, it's in the diary.

AMANDA: Never know with you.

GERALD: Of course I have.

GERALD pauses.

AMANDA: You know it's this one where we can find out whether it's a girl or a boy.

GERALD: No I don't think I did quite realise.

AMANDA: What do you think? Should we?

GERALD: Might as well. There's going to be enough surprises as it is.

GERALD carries on.

AMANDA: I've been thinking, you know what we should do.

GERALD: What's that?

AMANDA: We should have a party.

GERALD: That's more like it. Yes, definitely.

AMANDA: We could make it a party where we find out the sex of our baby.

GERALD: How do we do that?

AMANDA: We open the envelope that the doctor gives us in front of everyone and we all discover it together.

GERALD: It's ridiculous, sounds like a lot of fun though.

AMANDA looks excited.

AMANDA: And we should have pink champagne and blue curaçoa cocktails, and drink whichever is appropriate!

They both laugh.

GERALD: You really have thought this through haven't you? Let's do it properly though. I'll get Mark to do the catering. Get some invites printed, really make it into something.

AMANDA: How many should we invite?

GERALD: I don't know, thirty, forty?

AMANDA: Oh, a proper one.

They hug and kiss.

We're very lucky aren't we?

GERALD: We are, very lucky.

They kiss. GERALD looks at his watch.

AMANDA: You're going to be late.

GERALD: I'd better be off.

He hurriedly gets his things together.

AMANDA: Have a great day.

GERALD: You too. See you later.

AMANDA: Love you.

GERALD and AMANDA kiss, and hug goodbye.

CITY UNDERPASS

We are in a dingy inner-city thoroughfare. An underpass, it's dimly lit though, as such places tend to be.

Plenty of people are passing.

It's late but people are still on their way home from work.

KIERAN and JASON wait like hyenas looking on greedily at their potential prey.

The boys are observing everything closely. They look at particular people with real interest and resentment.

KIERAN: Look at this. Look at this.

JASON: Wow.

KIERAN: Sweet isn't it.

JASON: What's going on there?

KIERAN: Money's going on there, that's what's going on there.

JASON: It's looking good.

KIERAN: It's looking very good.

JASON: Give me the low-down. Give me your thoughts. Give me your wisdom. Just like you always do.

KIERAN: OK, listen up.

JASON: I love it when you do this bro, I just love it.

KIERAN: Rolex, I'd say it's a…yeah it's a Submariner. Gucci case, leather. Armani suit, definitely Armani. Ferrari C19 shades, tasty. Gold cufflinks, yeah gold cufflinks, Prada shoes, hardly worn, see look at the soles. He's had a manicure, check out his hands.

As he gets closer the observations are verified.

JASON: You are spot on bro. How the fuck do you do it?

KIERAN sniffs the air.

KIERAN: Ralph Lauren. Yeah, Safari.

JASON: Is it?

KIERAN: No mistaking.

JASON: You're a fucking genius.

KIERAN: He works somewhere top stuff. He is gold standard, total gold standard.

JASON: Give me more, go on. What's the other one?

KIERAN relishes this.

KIERAN: Omega watch, Hermes, Mulberry case, and that's a Burberry suit. These are classy. Total class.

JASON: Fuck we gotta take them, we've gotta have them.

KIERAN: Lives in Surrey or somewhere like that, he drives a Porsche, yeah a Porsche. A 911, it's sitting right now at Weybridge station waiting for him to get in it and go back to his nice detached house in a nice little country road.

JASON: How do you know this shit?

KIERAN: I just know. I've robbed from his sort. I've been up close and personal with his sort. I know where they're from, where they're going, and they are fucking pussies bro.

JASON: Do the valuation. Go on, the important bit.

KIERAN: Who him?

JASON: Yeah why not.

KIERAN: I reckon 15 grand, at least.

JASON whistles.

JASON: And to us?

KIERAN: We'd get between 5. Depending on what they've got in them bags. He's probably got a Vertu phone, those sort of fucks don't go out with your normal iPhone, there'll be an iPad, cash, some trinkets, oh fuck I'll say 10, we can make 5 grand out of them.

JASON: Let's do it. Let's just fucking do him. I want it, I want him.

JASON looks at KIERAN, looking for his wisdom, his feeling, his advice.

KIERAN: Yeah, but this man's clever, they don't go anywhere alone. We leave it. I don't like the smell of it.

Leave it.

JASON: I want that bitch with the Rolex, he's mine.

KIERAN stays firm.

KIERAN: Trust me bro, I've a got a feeling in my gut about them, and I don't like it, let them go.

JASON: Come on…

KIERAN: Trust me.

JASON: But…

KIERAN: Bro, just let them go.

KIERAN has to lay it on firmly, only then does JASON desist. They move onto other people.

Check this.

JASON: They are fully loaded.

KIERAN: Let's hear you, let's hear you for a change. Have a go.

JASON: Can I?

KIERAN: Let's see how good you are, see how well I've trained you.

JASON: D and G suit, yeah?

JASON looks to KIERAN for confirmation. KIERAN stays unmoved.

KIERAN: I'm listening bro, I'm listening.

JASON: Chanel bag, definitely, I know that.

JASON strains to see other stuff on her.

Oh yes, nice, she's got a Cartier watch. A fucking Cartier.

KIERAN: Which Cartier?

JASON: I don't know.

KIERAN: Not good enough. You got to know what it is. What model.

JASON: What is it then?

KIERAN: Tank Français. No mistaking it.

JASON is irritated at this.

Shoes?

JASON can't work them out.

JASON: No.

KIERAN: Choo. They are Choos, expensive shit.

JASON's trying to weigh it all up.

JASON: I reckon she's worth 10 grand?

KIERAN: Not bad. By the way it wasn't a Cartier at all, it was a Jaeger-LeCoultre.

JASON: Fucking wasn't.

KIERAN: I'm telling you bro it was. I know her, I know her sort. I know that watch.

JASON: Fuck.

KIERAN: It's alright, don't worry about it, it takes time to know these things.

A couple are walking along hand in hand. Young, in love, she leans into him. She is absorbed by him, and he by her.

He is aware and wary of KIERAN and JASON.

JASON: Look at these. Looks like a nice couple. They're in love.

KIERAN: That's right, she loves you, no one else fucking would.

JASON: Isn't it sweet.

KIERAN: He's a right pussy hole. What does she see in him.

JASON: She must love him.

KIERAN: Do you believe it? I don't believe it, I don't believe they love each other, I think she loves his money, and he loves her pussy.

JASON: Pretty good exchange, as far as I can see!

KIERAN: Yeah that's what it's all about isn't it, an exchange, a transaction, that's all anything is. There ain't no such thing as love.

JASON laughs, it's so outrageous.

JASON: You're twisted bro. You are really twisted, man. I love it.

It has become quieter. A lone businessman walks through the underpass.

KIERAN: Let's do this.

JASON: Let's do it.

KIERAN and JASON get into action. They do what they do well. They exact extreme violence very immediately.

They go back to the area we saw them in at the beginning of the scene. They become silhouetted again. Lights at the front fade out. The scene becomes dark and ultraviolet. Sounds of the violence fade up. AMANDA takes her place on the sofa again. Lights fade up on her.

GERALD AND AMANDA

GERALD is more distracted than normal today. His behaviour is noticeable.

GERALD: Morning.

AMANDA: Morning.

GERALD: I can't get used to you being up before me. It's weird. Herbal tea?

AMANDA smiles.

AMANDA: Got one.

GERALD: Sleepless night again?

AMANDA: Last night it felt like popcorn popping.

GERALD: Poor you.

GERALD gets buried in his Blackberry.

What have got on today?

AMANDA: I'm having lunch with Suzy.

GERALD: Oh good.

AMANDA: Haven't seen her for such a long time. Lots to catch up with, lots of gossip from work apparently. I thought we'd try somewhere different.

GERALD: For lunch?

AMANDA: Yeah, I was thinking of Pastorius.

GERALD: Um, I wouldn't, I think that place has had its day a bit. Why don't you try Ligeti? That new place everyone's talking about.

AMANDA: Won't it be completely booked out?

GERALD: I can get Lorraine on to it, she can get a table anywhere.

AMANDA: Would you?

GERALD: Course.

AMANDA: I might get some shoes and a dress while I'm out. There's that lunch on Saturday with Sarah and Michael.

GERALD: Oh fuck I forgot.

AMANDA: Don't swear.

GERALD: Sorry.

AMANDA: Baby will hear.

GERALD: At 20 weeks?

AMANDA: Yeah, they can hear. It affects them.

GERALD: I didn't realize.

AMANDA: It's OK.

GERALD: I'd completely forgotten about the lunch.

AMANDA: It was arranged weeks ago.

GERALD sighs.

GERALD: I've booked the trip.

AMANDA: What?

GERALD: The Gritti Palace.

AMANDA: When for?

GERALD: Next weekend.

AMANDA: You didn't say. We should have talked about it.

GERALD: I wanted it to be a surprise. I was going to tell you later.

AMANDA: Why later?

GERALD: Tonight.

AMANDA: You can't cancel it?

GERALD: I could. Of course I could. We just really need the break.

AMANDA: Do we?

GERALD: We do. You know we do. It's the Gritti Palace.

AMANDA sees how much it means to GERALD.

AMANDA: I'm sorry.

GERALD: It will be lovely, you know it will.

AMANDA: I'll tell them we can't make it.

GERALD: We can see them another weekend.

AMANDA: Are you OK?

GERALD: Yeah, fine, of course.

AMANDA: Are you sure?

GERALD: Yes.

AMANDA: You don't seem it.

GERALD: Big day at work.

AMANDA: I thought as much.

GERALD: Very big actually.

AMANDA: You never said.

GERALD: I don't say, you know I don't.

AMANDA: How big?

GERALD: Massive.

AMANDA: It's happening today?

GERALD: Yes.

AMANDA: I see, that's what Venice is about.

GERALD: No.

AMANDA: What time do you close?

GERALD: Three.

GERALD stands up. AMANDA considers all this.

Just have to hold my nerve.

AMANDA: You have doubts on this one?

GERALD: No, everything will fall into place. I'm set to make an awful lot of money today. A awful lot of money.

GERALD takes his time.

Think of me at three.

AMANDA: I will.

GERALD studies her.

Good luck today.

GERALD: Do you mean it?

AMANDA: I do, you know I do.

They kiss and hug.

KIERAN'S HOUSE

It is night time. We see KIERAN enter with JASON.

They have freshly returned from a robbery. They are flustered, but clearly high and psyched from what they have been doing.

KIERAN puts a carrier bag on the bed. JASON sits down. They are breathless from the excitement of their activities, still taking it all in. KIERAN paces around the room, full of adrenalin. He is like a wild animal.

JASON: You sure your mum's not here.

KIERAN: She won't be back until late. Don't worry the fuck about her.

JASON empties the contents of the bag onto the bed.

We see what comes out, a wallet, a couple of watches, a necklace, a couple of mobile phones, a Blackberry, an iPod, a purse, a small camera, some jewellery. Personal items that we all carry with us.

They both make satisfied noises as they see their haul.

Yes. Yes.

JASON: Nice one bro, nice one.

They inspect further.

Fuck. We did better than I thought.

They cackle over it all.

KIERAN: I did better you mean.
You just lurked in the background.

JASON: It's called watching your back, making sure you don't get nicked.

KIERAN: Is that right.

JASON: Fucking know that.

KIERAN smiles.

KIERAN: I'm just teasing you, you little pussy.

It is said affectionately. JASON doesn't mind.

KIERAN keeps sorting through the gear, he picks up a phone.

Look at this. Did you take this?

JASON: Yeah, it's Nokia 3040

KIERAN: What the fuck are you on, nicking a phone like this? What kind of a mug are you?

He takes the piss out of the phone.

And what kind of a pussyhole would carry around a slack phone like this anyway.

JASON: A loser bro, a fucking loser.

KIERAN: Good job I slapped him.

JASON laughs.

JASON: Fuck yes.

KIERAN is still obsessed with how poor the phone is.

KIERAN: He fucking annoyed me.

They laugh again.

JASON: Why did he put up a fight for it, that's what I want to know? Why would you put up a fight for that shit?

KIERAN scrolls through some of the contacts on the phone.

He looks at the photos of the victim's friends. He scoffs at them.

The image of a girl comes up.

KIERAN: Here look at this.

JASON: Tasty, bet that's his bitch.

KIERAN: You look nice don't you.

JASON: Bet he was fucking her.

He shows JASON the image. They laugh as they make further lewd noises.

KIERAN: I'd fuck her. That's for sure.

He scrolls through to the number, and looks at JASON, hoping he'll know what he thinks. They both twig what he's thinking. JASON's always a bit slower.

Let's have some fun.

KIERAN presses the call button.

Listen to this bro.

The girl answers. She's warm.

VOICE: Danny?

KIERAN puts on a voice.

KIERAN: Hello baby.

VOICE: Danny?

KIERAN: It's me baby.

VOICE: Danny??

KIERAN: I'm feeling really dirty tonight.

VOICE: What?

KIERAN: I want you to suck me off me baby.

KIERAN is trying to suppress his giggles throughout this.

VOICE: Who is this?!

KIERAN: It's Danny.

VOICE: Who are you? Where's Danny?

KIERAN starts laughing uncontrollably. His voice changes to KIERAN's again.

KIERAN: Danny's in hospital if he's got any fucking sense.

VOICE: Who are you?

KIERAN: Your worst fucking nightmare.

The phone goes dead. KIERAN phones it back straight away, he's in a mood now. Phone goes straight to answer-phone.

That makes it worse.

This is your warning, I'm out there, and I'm on you. You'd just better watch your back bitch. Your boyfriend or whatever he is, got what he deserved, and I did it, and I enjoyed it.

KIERAN takes the phone away from his face and shouts at it.

And he had a shit phone.

He throws the phone against the wall breaking it.

JASON looks a bit taken aback by the sudden escalation of violent behavior, but he's happy to join in with the tirade.

JASON: Yeah that's right K, you tell it how it is.

KIERAN gets back to business. It's like he's got work to do. He's now quicker and more agitated. His attention goes to the other items. He gets hold of the wallet. Goes through it, gets out the cash.

KIERAN: This is more like it.

He quickly takes out what he wants. The cash that is there.

Yeah, now this is me. This is definitely me. The money, always give me the fucking money.

KIERAN lights a spliff. He shares it with JASON.

Give that a go.

JASON takes it in.

KIERAN picks up the other bits and pieces. There's some money. He tallies it all up.

We'll get about a grand for the watch, 100 for the phone, 50 for the iPod, 150 for the iPad, and there's 120 cash here, that's about 1,420. Not bad. Not fucking bad for a day's work.

JASON doesn't seem to react.

I said it's not fucking bad, is it?

JASON: Yeah it's brill. I was just thinking though.

KIERAN: What were you thinking?

JASON: That's what he was worth to us, £1,420, I dunno, just a thought that came into my head.

KIERAN: Yeah, that's all he was fucking worth. You should stop thinking bro.

JASON: He was really properly fucking scared.

KIERAN: I like it when they're scared.

JASON: He was shitting himself.

KIERAN: He cried and whimpered. Like a fucking baby.

JASON: I thought you were going to fucking kill him for a minute. He was really bleeding. You had a rage going on bro, a proper rage.

KIERAN: Fuck yeah.

KIERAN darkens. JASON looks at him, like he's inspecting him.

JASON: You get a real buzz out of it don't you.

KIERAN: Of course I get a fucking buzz out of it.

JASON: Alright.

KIERAN looks at JASON, studies him.

KIERAN: You know why I get a buzz?

JASON: Come on you know what I mean, I'm just asking.

KIERAN: You don't know fucking anything do you.

JASON doesn't know what the right thing is to say.

There is an absolute madness in KIERAN's face now. He is overtaken by his aggression. KIERAN shouts in the way that he does when he robs, and it's very scary. It's as if he is going through the routine for himself as much as anything.

Let me tell you why I get a buzz. I get a buzz because I hate all these motherfuckers. I hate them with all my fucking heart. I like it when they get scared. It fucking turns me on bro when they get scared. It makes me more aggressive, and I like that in me. I want them to feel pain, I want to hurt them. It's my moment, my moment of fucking power. That's why I get a fucking buzz bro.

JASON is stunned by the outburst.

KIERAN looks at JASON.

You get me.

JASON: That's fucking hardcore bro. Hardcore.

GERALD breaks slowly into a big smile.

GERALD: I did it. I won. I've never seen a deal of this size go through so smoothly. Never. I can't describe how I'm feeling right now. Exhilarated. Maybe. It's all too much, too much. It's the biggest deal of my life.

Whilst he's talking AMANDA appears from behind; she stays there.

AMANDA: I know it's stupid, but I don't like to think about it.

GERALD: Think about what?

AMANDA: Nothing.

GERALD: Amanda?

AMANDA has great difficulty.

AMANDA: The money.

GERALD: What?

AMANDA: I know…

GERALD: The money? Are you serious?

AMANDA: It's just how I'm feeling.

GERALD: Where's all this come from?

AMANDA: I don't know. I'm thinking about us and what's around us, the times we live in.

GERALD: Times we live in… Fuck off. I don't believe I'm hearing this.

AMANDA: Please, I've told you, don't swear.

GERALD: You do like this life we have? This house?

AMANDA: Of course I do.

GERALD: Then you can't have it all ways. You can't have what we have, the life we have, the life we're going to have, without the money that I make.

AMANDA: I know.

GERALD: Please Amanda, think before you say this stuff.

AMANDA: Sometimes don't you think…

GERALD: What?

AMANDA: That we could live with just a bit less?

GERALD laughs.

GERALD: Darling, you don't know the concept of the word.

They both laugh.

You mean sell up? Sell this house? Sell the place in Painswick? Downsize? Is that what you mean?

AMANDA: We wouldn't have to do that?

GERALD: Get real Amanda. We would, we really would.

AMANDA can't respond.

It is you that wanted all this.

AMANDA: I know it is.

GERALD: I do as well, I know, I do. We agreed.

AMANDA: I know we did.

GERALD: It's why I do what I do.

GERALD cuddles AMANDA.

You need to know what my take is. What our take is. You need to know this.

AMANDA: I don't. Please don't.

GERALD: It's important you know.

AMANDA: It's not. I don't care.

GERALD: You do. It's important.

AMANDA: Leave it Gerald, OK.

GERALD starts to speak it to her. AMANDA covers her ears with her hands.

Please! No!

GERALD: Twenty.

AMANDA is shocked into silence. She takes her hands away from her ears. The silence pervades, reverberates.

Twenty fucking million.

GERALD nods at AMANDA's frozen face.

How do you feel now?

GERALD sounds like he's hyperventilating.

Tell me twenty million doesn't excite you. Go on, tell me. Tell me that doesn't change things.

GERALD looks at AMANDA, assessing her feelings.

AMANDA: Twenty million.

GERALD: Twenty million.

AMANDA: That's fucking insane.

GERALD: It's a serious amount of money.

AMANDA: Fuck.

GERALD: Now how do you feel? How do you feel about less now!

AMANDA: I don't know how I feel. I'm confused.

AMANDA is upset. GERALD takes hold of her. He comforts.

GERALD: I bet you are.

AMANDA: Twenty million.

AMANDA is clearly in a quandary.

GERALD: We'll have all our mortgages paid off. Done. School fees sorted for life. We can go wherever we want, whenever we want. We can do all that. This is for us and for our future, the future of our baby, and our children. This is important shit.

GERALD touches AMANDA's belly. It's an emotional moment.

GERALD comforts. They hug.

It's going to be OK. It really is.

Don't get upset.

Don't worry about anything. It'll get us confused. It's our world that matters. It's a good world that we are bringing our baby into. It's a good world, a very good world.

AMANDA: I'm probably just hormonal, the sleepless nights.

Back with KIERAN and JASON.

MUM: Kieran!

KIERAN: Fuck, hide it.

JASON: Fucking hell bro.

Just then the door opens, it's KIERAN's mum. KIERAN hides the stolen gear under the bed clothes.

MUM: Kieran, what the fuck is going on here? Why aren't you at jobseekers?

MUM sees JASON.

Who the fuck's this?

KIERAN: It's Jason.

MUM: And what the fuck is he doing here?

KIERAN: Just chilling mum.

MUM: You look guilty.

KIERAN: Guilty?

MUM: Yeah you do.

MUM looks around her, looks at things carefully. Looks at the bed. Sees something under it. Reveals it. She sees the haul.

What the fuck is this shit, all this stuff?

She starts to lose it.

Kieran what have you fucking done? You've fucking lied to me.

KIERAN: No.

MUM: Do you think I'm a cunt?

KIERAN can't answer, he is humbled.

I said, do you think I'm a cunt?

KIERAN: No, no way, of course not.

MUM: Then what the fuck are you doing? Fucking doing this, bringing all this shit in my yard.

KIERAN: We found it.

MUM: You didn't find this, you fucking stole it. I thought things were different, I thought you'd fucking changed.

KIERAN just looks guilty, the little boy in him comes out.

I told you I didn't want you robbing and thieving. We'll have the babylon round here again, and we don't need it. I don't want it, do you hear me?

KIERAN: Yeah.

MUM: Do you fucking hear me?

KIERAN: Yes I do mum.

MUM: Have you thought what will happen if you're caught this time?

KIERAN: No.

MUM: They'll fucking lock you up.

KIERAN: Yeah.

MUM: Is that what you want?

No answer.

Is it?

KIERAN: I don't care.

MUM: You fucking will care by the time I'm finished with you. Where's the money you've thieved?

KIERAN hesitates.

I want it.

KIERAN doesn't respond.

Give it to me, all of it.

KIERAN: I haven't got any.

MUM: Give me the fucking money.

She goes at him, hits him hard. He whimpers, he can't do anything about it. He relents.

KIERAN gets out his take. Hands it to his MUM.

Now get him out of here. I don't want trash like him in my yard.

KIERAN humbled, does as she says.

And take all this shit with you.

MUM leaves.

Transition.

KIERAN and JASON are together. Back in their usual territory. AMANDA is on the phone.

JASON: Why is she like that to you? Your mum.

KIERAN: Like what?

JASON: How she was.

KIERAN: And how was that?

JASON: I don't know.

There is genuine threat in KIERAN's tone. JASON looks away.

KIERAN: Go on, tell me.

JASON: She was really angry, I mean really angry.

KIERAN: She fucking hates me, fucking always hated me, and you know what. I fucking hate her too.

JASON: But she's still your mum.

We see GERALD in the background. He is on the phone to AMANDA. He now becomes part of the scene. The light comes up on him too now.

GERALD: Hey.

AMANDA: What's going on?

GERALD: It's been terrible traffic.

AMANDA: Everyone's here you know, we're waiting for you.

GERALD: I've just got out of the taxi, we were just sitting there for ages. Something's gone wrong, there must have been an accident or something.

AMANDA: How long are you going to be?

GERALD is flustered.

GERALD: I don't know where I am.

AMANDA: You don't know where you are?

GERALD: I'm on foot now.

AMANDA is concerned now.

AMANDA: You must know where you are.

GERALD: I think I recognise it.

AMANDA: Where did you get out of the taxi?

GERALD: The corner of Southampton Road. I'm just going to cut through some back streets. It won't take me long.

AMANDA: Gerald, I know that area. It's a bit dodgy.

GERALD: It's OK.

AMANDA: Shall I come and get you?

GERALD: I'll be fine.

AMANDA: I'm worried, come on. Let me.

GERALD: Don't worry. I'll be back before you know it. Amanda. I want you to know something.

AMANDA: What?

GERALD: I understand too you know. I understand how you feel. About money.

AMANDA: Do you?

GERALD: I know why you feel like that.

AMANDA: You said it was going to be OK.

GERALD: It will be. We're going to do something good with it too. We will.

AMANDA: Just hurry back OK?

GERALD: Apologize to everyone for me?

AMANDA: I will.

They stay frozen in their positions.

KIERAN: Tell me about your mum.

JASON: Come on.

KIERAN: No go on tell me. I told you, so you tell me.

JASON: There's nothing to say.

KIERAN: There must be, you got a mum haven't you? I've seen her.

JASON: Yeah.

KIERAN: Well then how is she?

JASON: She's alright.

KIERAN: She's alright is she. Normal is she?

JASON: Yeah.

KIERAN: Well good for you.

JASON: You know what I mean.

KIERAN: But she's there for you, yeah.

JASON: I suppose.

KIERAN: You're lucky, count yourself a lucky cunt.

GERALD: You know we really are very lucky.

AMANDA: I know, very lucky indeed.

GERALD: I really do I love you.

AMANDA: I love you too. Don't be long.

GERALD: You know I've got a feeling we'll be drinking blue curaçao all night.

AMANDA: Do you?

GERALD: Yeah.

AMANDA: Hurry back and let's find out.

GERALD: Bye.

> *GERALD looks around him again. He doesn't know where he is.*
>
> *He heads off in a direction he thinks will get him home.*
>
> *There is no one about to ask.*

It's not long before he becomes aware of KIERAN and JASON.

They are following close behind him.

GERALD stops. He turns round. He sees them. Turns and carries on walking.

Then he stops again and faces them in an attempt to make some normality of it.

You live around here?

KIERAN laughs at this.

KIERAN: Do I what?

GERALD: Do you live around here?

KIERAN: What?

KIERAN laughs with JASON again.

GERALD: OK.

GERALD turns his back again.

KIERAN: Yeah I do.

GERALD stops.

What's it to you?

GERALD: Nothing. Just.

KIERAN: Just what?

GERALD backs away.

OK bro let's see what we have here. That's an agnès b suit, stylish nice. He's got a Brietling, fuck let me take a look at that. Nice cufflinks, gold aren't they.

GERALD: What are you doing?

KIERAN: Just seeing what you're worth.

GERALD: What I'm worth?

JASON: Yeah what you're fucking worth.

GERALD: What are you worth then?

KIERAN laughs.

KIERAN: He thinks he's clever doesn't he.

A silence.

JASON: We're worth a whole lot more now you've turned up bro.

KIERAN: True, true.

GERALD: I just wanted some directions back to the main road, back to the Edgware Road, that's all, I know where I'm going from there.

KIERAN: Do you.

GERALD: Yes.

KIERAN stares unnervingly at GERALD.

Can you tell me the way?

KIERAN just looks.

To the Edgware Road?

KIERAN: I know what you are.

GERALD: OK you can't, fine.

GERALD starts walking again.

He stops dead in his tracks. He turns round.

KIERAN: You heard me. I know what you are, who you are, what sort you are.

GERALD: I just want to get home.

KIERAN: You're not going anywhere. I haven't given you permission.

GERALD: What?

KIERAN: I said I haven't given you permission.

GERALD: Don't be ridiculous.

KIERAN: You're mine now.

GERALD turns again and carries on walking, walks away, KIERAN bars his way.

I said you are not going anywhere.

GERALD looks down.

GERALD: For God's sake.

KIERAN imitates his voice, but in an exaggerated way.

KIERAN: For God's sake.

GERALD: I don't want any trouble.

KIERAN looks at JASON.

KIERAN: He doesn't want any trouble.

JASON laughs. JASON is more impatient.

JASON: Fucking do him. Fuck him up.

KIERAN studies GERALD, looks closely at his face. GERALD finds this completely unnerving.

KIERAN: You grew up in a nice part of London, didn't you, a nice, pretty, pretty, part. Didn't you?

JASON: The prettiest I bet.

GERALD looks incredulous.

KIERAN: You went to a nice expensive school didn't you. I know that too. Mummy and daddy paid for you all the way didn't they.

GERALD: You don't know me.

KIERAN: You've had all the chances in life, you've had all the breaks, haven't you?

GERALD: We all have a chance in life to do something, to be something. It doesn't matter where we come from, or what we have. You know that.

It's harder for some, less so for others.

KIERAN: It doesn't matter where you come from?? Who you fucking kidding? You telling me someone like you doesn't have it easier than a fuck from the estate like me? What are you talking about? Don't fucking insult me with such foolish talk.

JASON: Let me have a go.

KIERAN: Go on bro, show me what you can do.

JASON gets close to GERALD.

JASON: You live in one of those big motherfucking white houses that look all ornate, and newly painted, that have stairs going up to the front door, with big windows and expensive blinds with all nice things inside.

KIERAN: Nice bro, nice.

JASON: Bet you've got all the kit, all the best stuff, Bang and Olufsen, Poggenpohl, Starck.

KIERAN: You been doing your research, Poggenpohl, what the fuck's that?

JASON: It's a kitchen mate, don't you know anything.

KIERAN: Don't be fucking cocky.

GERALD: Who are you two?

KIERAN: Shut up…

KIERAN turns to GERALD again.

JASON: I look at those houses, I look at those lives, those people in those houses and you know what I wonder?

I wonder how they've got the fucking nerve to live right near me, near us, in our shit.

GERALD: Take it easy will you.

JASON: No I will not take it easy, why should I take it easy?

KIERAN: Fucking spot on though isn't he?

JASON: Am I?

KIERAN: You are bro.

GERALD: Look, you want money, is that what you want?

JASON: Yeah that's exactly what we want. Fucking money.

KIERAN keeps going with diatribe.

GERALD: You can have it, how much do you want?

GERALD goes to get out his wallet.

KIERAN: You know why I hate you?

GERALD: You don't hate me.

KIERAN: I hate you because you've got it all, and at the same time you're fucking people like me up with what you do. You are fucking this country aren't you. You are screwing everyone over and you don't give a fuck. You are ruining the planet, ruining humankind. You are the root of all evil, and you are the scum of the earth.

GERALD look at him incredulously.

GERALD: OK you've had your fun, now it's time to go.

KIERAN: You're not going anywhere.

There is a slight tussle as GERALD pushes to get away from KIERAN's grip.

GERALD: What do you want of me? For God's sake.

KIERAN: I haven't quite decided yet.

JASON: He's going to rob you, then bum you.

KIERAN laughs. He takes hold of GERALD's bag, opens it and sorts through the stuff in there, all the usual things.

KIERAN has been looking through GERALD's wallet.

He finds the envelope with the scanned picture of GERALD's baby.

KIERAN: What's this?

GERALD: Don't open that!

KIERAN: Why.

GERALD: Fucking don't, do you hear.

KIERAN does.

KIERAN: Sweet. You're going to be a daddy?

GERALD is upset.

Congratulations.

He finds cash, bank cards, etc.

Now this is what I want. I'll keep hold of all this.

KIERAN laughs as he starts to walk away. GERALD watches, battered.

GERALD: I bet your mum's really proud of you.

KIERAN stops in his tracks.

KIERAN: What did you say?

GERALD: I said I bet your mum is proud of you.

KIERAN: Don't talk about my mum. Don't you dare talk about my mum. Ever. OK.

KIERAN carries on walking.

GERALD: Does she know what you do?

He stops again.

KIERAN: You fuck.

GERALD: I bet if she knew she'd be ashamed.

KIERAN: Shut up.

KIERAN comes back.

GERALD: She doesn't know all this, does she.

KIERAN: Fucking well shut up, don't you talk about my mum. Shut up, shut up shut up.

GERALD: Have you even got a mum?

KIERAN: You fuck.

KIERAN draws his knife.

GERALD runs. They drop all the stuff on the ground.

KIERAN and JASON give chase.

They catch him quickly. KIERAN is full of hate. He stabs GERALD brutally.

KIERAN comes back and collects the bag and the wallet and the envelope with the scanned picture of GERALD's baby.

Fade to black. Time passing. Soundtrack.

Lights up.

KIERAN is with JASON. JASON has hold of an evening newspaper.

JASON: Gerald Collins, the financier who was murdered in Maida Vale on Monday aged 32, confounded the modern City stereotype.

KIERAN: From where I was standing he was the fucking stereotype. What are they talking about?

JASON: There's a whole load about him here, who he was, all that shit they write about someone when they're dead.

KIERAN: Read some more for me.

JASON: Not only was Gerald Ambrose a highly successful banker, he was also, both in his professional and personal life, a modest, gentle man of unshakable integrity.

KIERAN: He had integrity did he.

JASON: Collins was the head of corporate broking in mergers and acquisitions and had just been responsible for the takeover of British company Benson's, a deal reported to be worth 1.3 billion. You got hold of one here bro didn't you.

KIERAN: I choose well, see I told you, I can see it coming, I can smell it on them.

KIERAN smiles knowingly.

KIERAN laughs and JASON joins in, encouraging KIERAN further.

JASON: He was a trustee and chairman of a charitable joint venture which provides youth centres for deprived areas.

KIERAN: He gave away money when he wanted to. He should have given it all the time.

JASON: Those who came to know him well enjoyed his dry sense of humour, and respected and admired him as much as they liked him. Collins was devoted to his wife Amanda, who is expecting their first child.

KIERAN looks at JASON.

KIERAN: Bad luck his wife ever fucking met him.

KIERAN is different, harder now.

In a rage KIERAN rips the newspaper to shreds. Stamping on it. JASON joins in. They shout and scream abuse about the dead man. It's a full-on moment, full of excited hatred and hysterics.

JASON: You know all I want to do is be like you. You're the business. You're so fucking extreme.

KIERAN: Yeah well.

JASON: It's all I want. It's all that matters to me, to be like you.

KIERAN: You've got to think for yourself as well you know.

JASON: I don't need to though, all the while you're about, do I? And you're always going to be about aren't you?

The two sit in silence for a bit. The tone changes. JASON wants to get into something with KIERAN.

Bro?

KIERAN: Yeah?

JASON: What's it like to kill?

KIERAN: What?

JASON: Seriously.

KIERAN: What do you want to know for?

JASON: I don't know.

KIERAN changes.

He takes his time.

What did it feel like?

KIERAN: Nothing, it meant nothing, I felt nothing. Just hatred and anger in the moment. A madness. But there's no fucking feelings. Nothing at all.

JASON: What you feeling now?

KIERAN: Fuck all. Numb bro, completely fucking numb.

Just then GERALD approaches. No one can see him. He sits down next to KIERAN and observes him.

He gets out GERALD's wallet and sees a photo of AMANDA and the scanned photo of the baby.

GERALD comes up close. Still no one can see him.

KIERAN returns to the pictures of GERALD and AMANDA. GERALD sits down next to him and watches what he does, listens to what he says.

JASON: What's going on in your head?

KIERAN: I don't know, I'm thinking about what matters.

JASON: And?

KIERAN: I'm thinking bro, I'm thinking.

KIERAN snaps out.

JASON: And?

KIERAN: You know what, this matters.

KIERAN rifles through the things he took from GERALD's bag that are on the bed.

These things matter. Fuck do they matter.

JASON: That's more like it. Money, stuff, robbing, having, that's all that fucking matters. You're right, it's all that matters.

KIERAN: I don't give a fuck about anyone. I don't like anyone.

JASON: Nor do I, we're so fucking similar you and me.

KIERAN: Fuck everyone, fuck this city, fuck the world.

JASON: Yeah that's my Kieran, that's my fucking hero.

I'll see you later OK? We'll do some more shit later. Yeah?

KIERAN: Yeah bro, we really will.

JASON leaves. KIERAN is still there holding the wallet. He looks at it again. He looks at it carefully.

Who is there? There's someone there isn't there.

GERALD: It's me. I'm here.

KIERAN: What the fuck? You're dead, I killed you. You don't exist. What is this? Who the fuck are you?

GERALD: You know who I am.

KIERAN: But you're fucking dead. You are dead.

GERALD: Yes, you killed me, you murdered me.

KIERAN: This is crap.

GERALD: You murdered me. You stabbed me to death.

KIERAN: So?

GERALD: What you did was wrong, is wrong. It's the most basic wrong. Fucking well realise it, you piece of shit.

KIERAN: Fuck you.

GERALD: There are such things as right and wrong you know.

KIERAN: Are there?

GERALD: There really are.

KIERAN: What about you? Do you know that?

GERALD: Don't try and be clever.

KIERAN: I don't care about you. You're fucking nothing.

GERALD: That's where you're wrong, you see, I'm not nothing, not now I'm not. You'll never be rid of me, I'm always going to haunt you. I've got nothing else to do.

KIERAN: So fucking what.

GERALD: So I'm not nothing to you.

KIERAN: You are less than nothing, you always were, you always will be.

GERALD: Bollocks.

KIERAN: Believe it.

GERALD: You've got to live with what you've done.

KIERAN: You think I give a fuck?

GERALD: Yeah, because you're a human being, like we all are.

KIERAN: I'm not human though, enough people have said it. Therefore I feel nothing. I feel nothing for you or what I've done.

GERALD: Look at me and tell me you don't feel anything, with all honesty.

KIERAN looks deep into GERALD's eyes.

KIERAN: I don't feel anything. I feel nothing for you, or people like you. I don't feel anything for anyone. I don't think anyone is worth a toss in this life.

GERALD: There's a difference to what you say and what you really mean.

KIERAN: You're making me angry, you know what I'm like when I'm angry.

GERALD: You said you don't feel anything, being angry is a feeling.

KIERAN: Don't fuck with me.

GERALD: I am going to fuck with you.

KIERAN: I'm warning you, don't fuck with Kieran.

GERALD: Why? What's Kieran going to do? What can Kieran do?

KIERAN: I'll kill your fucking wife that's what I'll do.

GERALD: You really are despicable you know that.

KIERAN: You're the fucking fool in all this you know, and you got what you fucking deserved.

GERALD: Why did I deserve it?

KIERAN: Because you're one of them.

GERALD: One of who?

KIERAN: One of them who's got everything.

GERALD: And what's the difference eh? What's the real difference between you and me? I wanted it, I got it, you want it, and you're trying to get it. We're the same really aren't we, you and me. We both want money.

A moment between them.

You told me who I was, now I'm here to tell you who you are.

KIERAN: What?

GERALD: You have always been a pain in the arse to everyone that's ever known you, haven't you? You were useless at school, excluded, probably sent to a pupil referral unit. You were always in fights, never learning, never being interested in anything apart from robbing and thieving. You've always disliked everyone you've come into contact with. You've never achieved anything for yourself or anyone else. You don't want to, that's the thing, you don't want to, do you? Because you think that life has dealt you a bad hand, you blame everyone else for the situation you're in, and never think that you have to do anything about it yourself. You think that life owes you some debt. You can't keep girlfriends because you're abusive to them and can't offer them anything. The only thing that you believe in is the drugs that you buy with the money you take from thieving people like me. You are a disgrace, you know that don't you. You give nothing and take everything, and worse, you make people's lives a misery. That's what you do. That's what you are.

GERALD turns to the audience for this last bit.

I want my life back. I want what I had. I want to be with my wife. I want to see my baby born. Nothing else matters now. Nothing else.

The lights fade from GERALD at the front of the stage. GERALD walks off stage. Leaving KIERAN sat on the couch in a daze.

KIERAN's MUM appears.

MUM: Are you sick?

KIERAN doesn't respond.

You've done something haven't you.

I want you to find somewhere else to live, I don't want you here anymore. I've had it, I can't have you here anymore.

KIERAN stares at her disbelievingly.

You're never going to change. I can't do this with you anymore. You're no fucking good to me, I don't like how I am when you're around. I thought it was going to work, but it's not. All you've ever done is bring me misery, you always fuck everything up. Why do you think your father left? It was because of you. I don't want anyone else leaving because of you. Just get yourself together and do what I want. Fucking well do what I want. You hear.

KIERAN gets up and walks out.

FRONT ROOM

We are with AMANDA.

There is a ring at the door.

AMANDA answers. It is KIERAN. AMANDA doesn't know what to make of this. She doesn't know him of course. It feels strange, odd. We really don't quite know what is going to happen, is he there to kill her? It is full of tension.

AMANDA looks at him full of a strange curiosity.

KIERAN: Mrs Ambrose?

AMANDA: Yes.

    AMANDA nods. She's desperately trying to work the situation out.

    Who are you?

KIERAN: I'm Kieran.

    He offers his hand to shake.

    AMANDA nods.

AMANDA: What do you want?

    KIERAN seems silenced.

    Well?

    Still nothing.

    I'm sorry I'm really quite busy.

    She goes to shut the door.

KIERAN: Please. Listen.

AMANDA: I'm sorry, I can't do this.

KIERAN: It's about your husband.

    AMANDA is rooted to the spot.

    I saw what happened.

AMANDA seems dazed. Stunned. KIERAN is affected by AMANDA's reaction.

AMANDA: Have you been to the police?

KIERAN: No.

AMANDA: Why not?

KIERAN: I wanted you to know first.

AMANDA doesn't quite know what to do. She looks at him intently.

AMANDA: I don't understand. How do you know where I live.

KIERAN: I found this nearby. That's how I know you.

KIERAN produces the wallet. He offers it to her. AMANDA takes it and holds it preciously. She is lost in it, and in the moment. There is something about this which totally floors her.

Are you alright?

KIERAN looks down as AMANDA starts to cry. She pulls herself together.

AMANDA: Where was it?

KIERAN: I found it, on the pavement.

AMANDA gets herself together.

AMANDA: How come you were there?

KIERAN: It's my manor.

AMANDA: You live there?

KIERAN: Yeah.

AMANDA: What exactly did you see??

KIERAN: You don't want to know.

AMANDA: I do, I need to know.

KIERAN: It's not why I'm here.

AMANDA: Please tell me.

KIERAN: You really want to know?

AMANDA: I do.

KIERAN gets himself together.

KIERAN: I heard shouting. I could tell it was a robbery. They were trying to get his case from him. He wasn't letting them, it was getting bad. He just wouldn't let go. Then I saw him fall to the ground.

AMANDA: You saw it going on?

KIERAN: Yes.

AMANDA: And you saw Gerald?

KIERAN: Yes.

AMANDA: Oh my God. You're a witness? Why haven't you been to the police? There have been all kinds of appeals for witnesses. I don't understand.

KIERAN: I don't trust the police, I'd be framed or something.

AMANDA: What about when it was going on, why didn't you call them then?

KIERAN: Just doesn't happen round our way. No one would do that.

AMANDA: What??

KIERAN: No one trusts the police. They'd bang any of us up for nothing.

AMANDA: Even when someone's being murdered!

KIERAN: I didn't know that did I.

AMANDA: You stood by and saw this?

KIERAN: It wasn't like that.

AMANDA: What the fuck was it like then?

KIERAN turns.

KIERAN: Don't fuck with me. OK.

AMANDA: Why? What are you going to do?

KIERAN: I tell you what I'm going to fucking do.

AMANDA: Yes? Go on, tell me.

KIERAN backs down, he subsides.

KIERAN: It's life on the estate. You don't get involved, you don't understand.

AMANDA: Gerald was just left there?

KIERAN: Yeah.

AMANDA: Was he dead?

KIERAN bows his head.

AMANDA looks back at the wallet.

KIERAN is drinking all this reaction in. It is affecting him. AMANDA gets herself together again.

KIERAN is more uncomfortable.

AMANDA: How could anyone kill someone?

KIERAN stumbles at this point. He shakes his head.

Why?

KIERAN: There are desperate people out there, people who would do anything. Anything to make a few quid.

AMANDA: But to kill?

KIERAN: When someone's got nothing. Nothing in their life.

AMANDA: It doesn't fucking matter. I want whoever did it to be found.

KIERAN: You must hate them.

AMANDA: They have to live with what they have done.

KIERAN considers this.

They need to see the hurt they've caused. They need to face me, they are going to face me.

KIERAN: Why do you want to face them?

AMANDA: So I can understand.

KIERAN: I can't imagine how you're feeing.

AMANDA: He was everything, my life, my world. He was the reason for everything. We are expecting a baby. You know that?

KIERAN shakes his head. He gets out the envelope with the scanned picture in it. He gives it to her.

KIERAN: I found this too.

AMANDA is affected. She opens the envelope and looks at the scan.

AMANDA: We so wanted this baby. I'll probably have a fucking miscarriage now. It's all so fucked. What am I going to do?

KIERAN: You got to stay strong.

AMANDA: Why?

KIERAN: For your baby.

AMANDA: What's the point now.

KIERAN: Because you have to. You have to be there for your baby. It's important. It's the most important thing ever.

AMANDA: You don't know what it feels like.

KIERAN: I know I don't, but there are certain things I do know.

Just then they touch. There is something in it. An unusual moment. KIERAN is embarrassed. AMANDA holds his hand to comfort and for comfort.

Your baby is going to be a very lucky baby. To have you as a mother.

AMANDA: That's a lovely thing to say.

KIERAN: You will be a good mother I know.

AMANDA: I'll be like every mother.

AMANDA is touched. A tear comes to her eye.

I'm going to be like most people, I'll be like most mothers, it's actually all I've ever really wanted.

KIERAN turns to go. Then turns back.

KIERAN: You said that you wanted to meet the killer of your husband. To face him. To look him in the eyes?

AMANDA: More than anything. It's the only way I'll find peace.

KIERAN turns and faces her.

THE STREETS

We are back in the workplace of KIERAN and JASON. They are back on the streets again.

People pass. KIERAN is silent, distracted. He has his packed bag with him.

JASON: I love this.

KIERAN doesn't respond.

Fucking love it.

KIERAN looks blankly ahead.

Look at them all, all of them ours.

KIERAN looks down.

OK here we go. Here's some likely victims. He's got a tag, Hermès suit, Guccis on the feet, he's got a Dunhill case, yeah a Dunhill, tasty. Fuck he is loaded bro. Loaded. What do you reckon, not bad going eh? Come on let's hear you. Your words, your thoughts, your poetry, your ideas. You know how I love it.

Silence.

Come on, I'm waiting.

Silence. KIERAN stares into space.

Bro what's going on?

Nothing.

Bro?!

GERALD slowly has arrived and is there watching everything.

KIERAN: I'm not feeling it.

JASON: Come on bro.

KIERAN: You stupid fuck, you don't get it do you?

KIERAN walks away.

JASON: Where are you going? You can't leave me, what am I going to do? It's no good without you.

KIERAN: Then do something else.

JASON: What can I do?

KIERAN: You're on your own.

JASON: Don't leave me. Don't do this to me. Don't go. It's all I know. Don't leave me, don't abandon this. We got to keep this going. We've got to keep taking, and making and fucking people up, we've got to!

KIERAN: You get a real buzz out of it now, don't you.

JASON: Course I get a fucking buzz. Let me tell you why I get a fucking buzz. I get a buzz because I hate all these motherfuckers. I hate them with all my fucking heart. I like it when they get scared. It fucking turns me on bro when they get scared. It makes me more aggressive, and I like that in me. I want them to feel pain, I want to hurt them. It's my moment, my moment of fucking power. That's why I get a fucking buzz bro.

KIERAN leaves JASON there.

The scene fades to black.

WWW.OBERONBOOKS.COM